# Crèmes brûlées

Use Mastrad cooking torches to prepare your crèmes brûlées!

Go beyond simple caramelized crème brûlée and create your very own appetizers and starters, side dishes and mini oven desserts to enchant your guests!

Hot, cold, sweet or savoury: crèmes brûlées, the sweetest of sins...by far!

Your guests will go crazy for them!

Simple and quick! Discover the pleasure of crèmes brûlées! As a starter, side dish or dessert of course, these recipes open the door to: melt in the mouth creams, crunchy caramel, intense flavours and spices.

You'll easily be able to make and create your very own crèmes brûlées recipes.

Jean-Claude Fascina
Consultant chef

Photographs by Julien Bouvier

I

# Crèmes brûlées with a cooking torch

To be just as successful as an experienced chef when making crèmes brûlées, all you have to do is follow our practical advice.

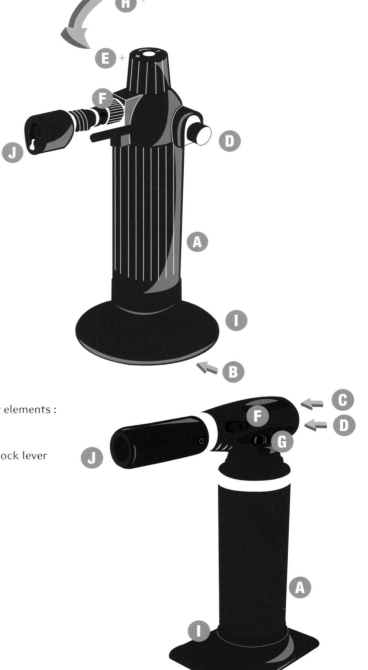

# Cooking torches

Mastrad proposes 2 cooking torches: a regular model and a professional model.

Simple to use, the cooking torches are made up of the following elements :

- **A** Gas chamber
- **B** Filler valve
- **C** Safety lock
- **D** Piezzo ignition
- **E** Gas release knob
- **F** Flame adjustment slide
- **G** Continuous flame lock lever
- **H** On/ off
- **I** Removable base
- **J** Knozzle
- **K** Lighter fuel

# Advice for use

1 – Before use, ensure that the cooking torch has cooled down: always wait 30 minutes between each use.

2 – With the cooking torch turned off: fill the gas chamber **A** with lighter fuel **K** through the filler valve **B** hold the torch upside down, away from heat, then leave to stand for 2 minutes.

3 – Sprinkle the topping (sugar etc...) over the top of the dish.

4 – Professional model: release safety lock **C** ;
Regular model, turn gas release knob to **E** +.

5 – Hold the cooking torch away from any material or flammable objects and push the piezzo ignition **D**.

6 – Adjust the gas flow **E** on the regular model. On the professional model, push the continuous flame lock lever **G**. Hold the torch about 10 cm away from topping.

7 – Depending on the topping, choose the intensity: high or low flame intensity **F** :
  - Sugars: maximum intensity - blue flame
  - Biscuits, herbs, gingerbread, olive paste, breadcrumbs, hard breads sticks: medium intensity - yellow flame

8 – Ensure even surface cooking by making circular movements over the topping until required browning is obtained.

9 – Heat the crèmes one after the other.

10 – Turn off the cooking torch **H** - **D** leave to stand upright on removable base **I**.

11 – Do not store near heat sources.

Carefully read the instruction booklet included, before using your cooking torch.

# For an incredibly creamy & delicious crème

All crèmes brûlées are made from a basic mixture of egg yolks, fresh cream and milk.

To ensure your crèmes brûlées' creaminess and «melt in the mouth» texture, you should use full fat fresh cream, mascarpone or full fat cream mixed with ricotta or yoghurt.

To add subtle flavours to your crèmes brûlées, flavour the milk and cream with herbs, tea, flowers, spices or oily elements (bacon, salmon).

For enhanced flavours add blended, sieved elements to the cream.

To surprise the palate and vary textures, add small pieces of vegetable, bacon, seafood, mushroom or fruit to the cream – be sure to drain before adding.

Cook the crèmes in a double boiler in a pre-heated oven.

For cold recipes, leave to cool at room temperature then place in the fridge for at least 2 hours before adding the topping and caramelizing.

## Varied toppings

The traditional crunchy caramel topping is made with brown sugar, but it can be flavoured using the many varieties of flavoured sugars found in gourmet food stores (lavender, vanilla, sweets...) or you can simply use crushed sour boiled sweets.

Caramel can also be used with sweet & sour mixes.

Try varying the toppings by using crumbled biscuits, powdered dried fruits, gingerbread, breadcrumbs, chopped herbs, pastry filled with olive paste, etc.

## Crèmes brûlées conservation

Crèmes brûlées can be kept, uncovered, in the fridge for 48 hours.

Only caramelize when ready to serve.

# Cold

As appetizers or starters, these cold savoury crèmes brûlées will delight guests at your parties!
Simple to make, they are incredibly refined and melt in the mouth, bringing together subtle textures
and flavours, worthy of the very best restaurants.
Prepare your crèmes beforehand and use the cooking torch to add the finishing touch when ready to serve…
A true delight for the eyes and taste buds!

cold

# Crème brûlée with foie gras and pine nuts

## Ingredients

150g/ 5 ¼ oz raw duck foie gras

6 egg yolks

50cl/ 17 fl oz semi-skimmed milk

15g/ ½ oz unsalted butter

50g/ 1 ¾ oz pine nuts

6 teaspoon brown sugar

Salt, ground black pepper

6 ramekins or 24 mini ramekins

1 Pre-heat the oven to 160°C/ 320°F.
Cut the raw foie gras into small pieces and remove any veins.

2 Pour the milk into a blender, add the pieces of foie gras and mix thoroughly until you obtain a smooth creamy mixture.

3 Gradually add the egg yolks, season with salt and pepper.

4 Pass the ramekins under hot running water, dry and grease with butter.
Fill with the cream foie gras.

5 Place the ramekins in the drip pan, pour some cold water in the drip pan and place in the oven in a double boiler for 30 minutes for the ramekins, 15 minutes for the appetizers.

6 At the end of the cooking time, remove the ramekins and leave to cool for 30 minutes, before placing in the fridge for at least 3 hours.

7 When serving, crush the pine nuts and mix them with the brown sugar in a small bowl. Sprinkle this mixture over the crème brulée and caramelize with a cooking torch.
Eat straight away.

| 4 starters | ou | 16 appetizers | preparation 25 mn leave to stand 2 h | starters 160°C Th 5 30 mn | mini oven 160°C Th 5 15 mn | difficulty ★★★ |

# Crème brûlée with pepper & provencal-style bread sticks

## Ingredients

4 egg yolks

20cl/ 8 ½ fl oz full milk

20cl/ 8 ½ fl oz single cream

1 red pepper

1 sprig thyme

4 slices brown bread

2 tablespoons brown sugar

1 tablespoon tapenade (black olive paste)

Olive oil

Salt, ground pepper


1 fine sieve

1 Mastrad steamer

4 ramekins or 16 serving spoons

1 Pre-heat the oven to 160°C/ 320°F.

2 Peel the pepper, remove the seeds and dice. Cook in the steamer with a drizzle of olive oil for 5 minutes in a 700W microwave on a medium heat or for 15 minutes in the oven on 160°C/ 320°F.

3 Pour the milk and the chopped pepper in a blender, season with salt and pepper. Mix thoroughly and pour through a fine sieve.

4 In a round bottomed bowl, whisk the egg yolks and thyme leaves. Add the cream and pepper mixture. Mix thoroughly.

5 Share the mixture between the ramekins (or serving spoons), place them in the drip pan and pour some warm water inside. Place in the oven in the double boiler: for 30 minutes for the ramekins, 15 minutes for the serving spoons.

6 Remove the crèmes from the oven and leave to cool at room temperature before placing in the fridge for at least 2 hours.

7 Slice the brown bread into sticks, brown them quickly in a pan with some olive oil, spread some tapenade (black olive paste) on them and put to one side.

8 When ready to serve, sprinkle the crèmes with brown sugar and caramelize with the cooking torch. Eat with the tapenade covered bread sticks

## Chef's tips

Mastrad's thin skin Elios® peeler is perfect for peeling the pepper.

4 people

preparation
30 mn

leave to stand
2 h

160°C Th 5
30 mn

difficulty
★ ★ ★

# Light crème brûlée on a bed of courgette with crispy filo triangle

## Ingredients

6 egg yolks

40cl/ 13 ½ fl oz soy cream

1 medium/ or 2 small courgettes

1 small shallot

5 fresh basil leaves

1 sheet filo pastry

1 pinch ground cumin

1 tablespoon brown sugar

Olive oil

Salt, ground pepper


4 deep ramekins

1  Pre-heat the oven to 160°C/ 320°F.
Peel and chop the shallot.
Wash the courgettes and cut into thin slices.
Chop the basil leaves.

2  Heat a drizzle of oil in a pan and brown the courgettes and the shallot.
Be sure to keep them crunchy.

3  In a round bottomed bowl, beat the egg yolks, season with salt and pepper.
Add the soy cream, chopped basil and mix together gently.

4  Cover the bottom of the ramekins with the slices of courgette and the shallot.
Pour the mixture over the vegetables.

5  Place the ramekins in an ovenproof dish and fill it with warm water up to ⅔ of the dish
height. Place in the oven in a double boiler for 30 minutes.

6  Whilst the crèmes cook, cut the sheet of filo pastry into 4 triangles.
Brown them slightly in a pan with a little olive oil and sprinkle ground cumin and salt
over the top. Put to one side.

7  Remove the ramekins from the oven and leave to cool at room temperature before placing
in the fridge for at least 2 hours.

8  When ready to serve, sprinkle the crèmes with brown sugar and caramelize with
the cooking torch and decorate with a cumin filo triangle.

## Chef's tips

This light crème brulée will delight all those keeping tabs on their waistline!

| 4 starters | ou | 16 appetizers | preparation 20 mn leave to stand 2 h | starters 120°C Th 4 40 mn | mini oven 120°C Th 4 20 mn | difficulty ★ ★ ★ |

# Crème brûlée with asparagus & truffle curls

## Ingredients

4 egg yolks

20cl/ 6 ¾ fl oz milk

20cl/ 6 ¾ fl oz single full fat cream

1 bunch green asparagus

1 small, canned, black truffle

1 tablespoon brown sugar

Salt, ground pepper

1 fine sieve

4 ramekins or 16 mini ramekins

1 Pre-heat the oven to 120°C/ 248°F. Boil a large pan of salted water.

2 Wash and peel the asparagus.
Plunge them into the boiling water and leave to cook for 8 minutes. Drain.
Keep 4 asparagus spears for decoration and chop the rest.

3 Pour the milk in a blender. Add the chopped asparagus, add pepper and adjust the salt, if necessary.
Mix thoroughly, until you obtain a creamy mixture. Pour the mixture through a fine sieve.

4 In a round bottomed bowl, whisk the egg yolks, season with salt and pepper.
Add the fresh cream, the truffle juice and the asparagus cream. Mix together gently.

5 Share the mixture between the ramekins. Place the ramekins in an ovenproof dish and add some water. Place in the oven in a double boiler for 30 minutes for the ramekins and 15 minutes for the appetizers.

6 In the meantime: for the appetizers: cut the asparagus spears in 4, lengthways.
Open the oven, delicately place the spears on top of the crèmes and leave to cook: for 10 minutes for the ramekins and 5 minutes for the appetizers.

7 Leave to cool at room temperature then place in the fridge for at least 2 hours.

8 When ready to serve, sprinkle the crèmes with brown sugar and caramelize with the cooking torch. Using a grater or peeler, make thin curls of truffle and place them on top of the crèmes brûlées.

## Chef's tips
Mastrad's thin skin Elios® peeler is perfect for making the truffle curls.

# Crème brûlée with ricotta & wild rocket

## Ingredients

6 egg yolks

20cl/ 6 ¾ fl oz full fat milk

30g/ 1 ¼ oz drained ricotta cheese

100g/ 3 ½ oz wild rocket

1 tablespoon pine nuts

1 tablespoon brown sugar

1 pinch Cayenne pepper

Olive oil

Salt, ground pepper


1 fine sieve

1 square Mastrad papillote or round steamer

4 x 125g/ 4 ½ oz small glass jars

1. Pre-heat the oven to 160°C/ 320°F.

2. Wash and dry the rocket. Cook it in a steamer with a drizzle of olive oil for 30 seconds in a microwave or 5 minutes in the oven at 160°C/ 320°F.

3. Pour this compote into a blender. Add the milk and a pinch of Cayenne pepper. Mix thoroughly and pour through a fine sieve.

4. In a round bottomed bowl, beat the egg yolks and the ricotta. Gradually add the milk-rocket mixture, stirring as you do so. Adjust the seasoning if necessary.

5. Share the mixture between the glass jars, place them in an ovenproof dish and add warm water up to ⅔ of the height of the jars. Place in the oven in a double boiler for 25 minutes.

6. Whilst the crèmes cook, roast the pine nuts in a pan without any oil.

7. Remove the jars from the oven and leave to cool at room temperature before placing in the fridge for at least 2 hours.

8. When ready to serve, sprinkle the crèmes with brown sugar and pine nuts and caramelize with the cooking torch.

## Chef's tips

This cold crème brûlée can be eaten as a starter or as a main dish accompanied with a rocket salad, seasoned with balsamic vinegar.

16 appetizers

preparation 20 mn
leave to stand 2 h

140°C Th 3
20 mn

difficulty
★ ★ ★

cold

# Crème brûlée with mascarpone & walnuts

## Ingredients

4 egg yolks

20cl/ 6 ¾ fl oz full fat milk

15cl/ 2 fl oz full fat single cream

30g/ 1 ¼ oz mascarpone cream

20g/ ¾ oz walnuts

2 tablespoons brown sugar

Walnut oil

Salt, ground pepper

16 mini ramekins
or serving spoons

1  Pre-heat the oven to 140°C/ 284°F.

2  Pour the water into the pan and add the cream and whisk together.
Cook on a low heat, stirring continuously.
Add a drizzle of walnut oil and leave to infuse for 15 minutes.

3  In a round bottomed bowl, whisk the egg yolks and the mascarpone,
season with salt and pepper.
Gradually add the, still warm, infused milk gently mixing with a silicone spoon
– without frothing. Adjust the seasoning.

4  Share the mixture between the mini ramekins or serving spoons and place them
in the drip pan. Pour cold water into the pan and put in the oven in a double boiler
for 20 minutes.

5  Leave to cool at room temperature then place in the fridge for 2 hours.

6  Crush the walnuts.

7  When ready to serve, sprinkle the crèmes with brown sugar and walnuts and caramelize
with the cooking torch.

| 4 people | preparation 30 mn | | difficulty |
|---|---|---|---|
| | leave to stand 2 h | 100°C Th 3 60 mn | ★ ★ ★ |

# Crème brûlée with lentils on slices of foie gras

## Ingredients

4 egg yolks

4 x 20g/ ³/₄ oz slices raw foie gras

20cl/ 6 ³/₄ fl oz full fat milk

20cl/ 6 ³/₄ fl oz full fat cream

50g/ 1 ³/₄ oz lentils

1 shallot

1 small carrot

2 sprigs parsley

2 tablespoons granulated sugar

Grapeseed oil

Salt, ground pepper

4 small ceramic cocottes
(or terra cotta dishes)

1 Pre-heat the oven to 100°C/ 212°F.
Wash, dry and chop the parsley. Put to one side.

2 Peel the carrot and shallot and dice.
Pour a little olive oil in a thick based pan.
Brown the vegetables for a few minutes.

3 Add the lentils to the vegetables. Mix together quickly and add twice their volume in water, season with salt and pepper, and leave to cook on a low heat for 15 minutes.

4 In a round bottomed bowl, whisk the egg yolks, the milk and cream.
Gently add the lentil mixture. Add the chopped parsley and stir gently.

5 Season the slices of foie gras with salt and pepper. Place them at the bottom of the cocottes and cover with the lentil mixture.

6 Place the cocottes in an ovenproof dish, pour cold water in the dish up to ²/₃ of the cocottes' height and place in the oven in a double boiler for 60 minutes.

7 Leave the cocottes to cool at room temperature before placing them in the fridge for 2 hours.

8 When ready to serve, sprinkle the crèmes with brown sugar and caramelize with the cooking torch. Eat straight away.

## Chef's tips

Use this recipe to contrast textures: the «melt in the mouth» aspect of the foie gras, the smoothness of the crème brûlée, the crispy caramel and crunchy lentils.

| 6 people | preparation 10 mn | <br>160°C Th 5 | difficulty |
|---|---|---|---|
| | leave to stand 2 h | 25 mn | ★ ★ ★ |

# Crème brûlée with sundried tomatoes & parmesan

## Ingredients

150g/ 5 ¼ oz sundried tomatoes in oil

75cl/ 25 ¼ fl oz thick fresh cream

2 egg yolks

6 parmesan curls

3 cherry tomatoes

6 sprigs chives

Slightly salted butter

2 tablespoons brown sugar

Salt, ground pepper

6 ovenproof glasses

1 Pre-heat the oven to 160°C/ 320°F.
Drain the sundried tomatoes.

2 In a blender, mix the sundried tomatoes with the cream and egg yolks, season with salt and pepper.

3 Run the ovenproof glasses under hot water, dry and lightly butter them.

4 Place a curl of parmesan at the bottom of each glass.

5 Share the mixture between the glasses.

6 Place the glasses in an ovenproof dish. Pour cold water in the dish up to ⅔ of the glasses' height and place in the oven in a double boiler for 25 minutes.

7 Remove the glasses from the oven and leave to cool at room temperature.
Put them in the fridge for at least 2 hours.

8 When ready to serve, sprinkle the crèmes with brown sugar and caramelize with the cooking torch. Decorate each crème brûlée with half a cherry tomato and a sprig of chives.

## Chef's tips

Eat as a starter, accompanied with a rocket salad.
Eat whilst warm, this recipe is perfect with roast fish or spicy prawns.

# Hot

Add a touch of originality to your starters and side dishes
with these hot crèmes brûlées and blow your guests taste buds!
Both smooth and crunchy: close your eyes, sit back and delight in this gourmet melting moment !

| 4 people | preparation 25 mn | 160°C Th 5 20 mn | difficulty ★ ★ ★ |
|---|---|---|---|

# Crème brûlée with mussels & turmeric

## Ingredients

12 mussels (in shells)

125ml/4 ½ fl oz full fat milk

2 sprigs flat parsley

3 egg yolks

1 pinch turmeric

1 pinch mixed spices

1 tablespoon fresh cream

1 tablespoon breadcrumbs

1 tablespoon granulated sugar

Salt, ground pepper

1 fine sieve

4 small ovenproof dishes

1 Pre-heat the oven to 160°C/ 320°F.
Chop the parsley.

2 Clean the mussels.
In a thick bottomed pan, heat them for a few minutes, until they open slightly.
Place a fine sieve over a round bottomed bowl. Pour the contents of the pan through the sieve to filter off the juice from the mussels. Put the mussels to one side.

3 Beat the egg yolks with the juice form the mussels, season with salt and pepper.

4 Pour the milk in a pan and heat gently.
Add the chopped parsley, fresh cream and turmeric.
Whisk into the eggs, vigorously.

5 Remove the mussels' shells and share them between the small ovenproof dishes.
Gently pour the mixture over the mussels.

6 Place the ovenproof dishes in the drip pan, pour some warm water inside and place in the oven in a double boiler for 20 minutes.

7 Remove the ovenproof dishes from the oven and leave to stand for 5 minutes.
In the meantime, mix together the granulated sugar, breadcrumbs and mixed spices.
Sprinkle this mixture over the crèmes and caramelize with the cooking torch.
Serve straight away.

## Chef's tips

This recipe can be used to make 16 apetizers.
In this case, reduce the cooking time by half.

**4 people** | preparation **15 mn** | 120°C Th 4 **30 mn** | difficulty ★★★

# Tajine-style crème brûlée with dried fruit

## Ingredients

6 egg yolks

150ml/ 5 ¼ fl oz semi-skimmed milk

50ml/ 1 ¾ fl oz full fat cream (minimum 35% fat content)

2 dried figs

2 dried apricots

8 raisins

1 tablespoon grated parmesan

1 tablespoon brown sugar

1 teaspoon tajine spices

1 pinch Cayenne pepper

Virgin olive oil

Salt, ground pepper


4 mini tajines dishes

1 Pre-heat the oven to 120°C/ 248°F.
Cut the dried figs and apricots into small pieces.

2 In a round bottomed bowl, beat the egg yolks with a pinch of salt and a twist of ground pepper. Add the cream and whisk together until smooth. Add a drizzle of olive oil and mix.

3 In a pan, boil the milk along with the spices and the Cayenne pepper. Gradually pour the hot, spiced milk over the egg and cream mixture, whisking as you do so.

4 Share the dried fruits between the mini-tajine dishes then cover with the hot mixture. Place the mini-tajine dishes in the drip pan, pour some water inside and place in the oven in a double boiler for 30 minutes.

5 Remove the tajine dishes from the oven, sprinkle with grated parmesan and some brown sugar. Caramelize with the cooking torch and serve straight away, with the lid on.

## Chef's tips

The perfect side dish to grilled lamb or roast chicken.

# Crème brûlée with carrots & mustard grain

## Ingredients

4 egg yolks

20cl/ 6 ¾ fl oz milk

20cl/ 6 ¾ fl oz full fat cream

2 carrots

1 tablespoon mustard grains

1 tablespoon brown sugar

Salt, ground pepper

1 silicone Mastrad steamer

1 fine sieve

4 ovenproof glass jars or individual ramekins

1 Pre-heat the oven to 120°C/ 248°F.

2 Wash and peel the carrots, slice thinly and cook in a silicone steamer with 2 tablespoons of water for 4 minutes in a 700W microwave or in a traditional oven for 12 minutes at 160°C/320°F.

3 Pour the milk into a blender. Add the carrots and mix thoroughly. Pour the mixture through the sieve.

4 In a round bottomed bowl, whisk the egg yolks, season with salt and pepper. Gradually add the cream, followed by the carrot mixture, mix gently.

5 Share the carrot cream between the ovenproof glasses and place in a dish in the oven. Pour warm water in the dish up to ⅔ of the glasses height and place in the oven in a double boiler for 30 minutes at 120°C/ 248°F.

6 Remove from the oven, sprinkle with brown sugar and caramelize with the cooking torch. Sprinkle mustard grains over the top. Serve straight away.

 Chef's tips

Vary the grains used: replace the mustard with poppy seeds or cumin which also go well with carrots.

| 4 people | preparation 30 mn | 160°C Th 5 30 mn | difficulty ★★★ |

# Cod brandade crème brûlée with purple potato chips

## Ingredients

2 egg yolks

20cl/ 6 ¾ fl oz semi-skimmed milk

100g/ 3 ½ oz desalted cod filet

1 charlotte potato

1 vitelotte potato

1 clove garlic

1 small sprig parsley

2 tablespoons oil – grapeseed for example

1 tablespoon brown sugar

Salt, ground pepper

1 colander

4 individual ovenproof dishes

1 Wash the charlotte potato and cook in a pan of salted water for 20 minutes, start with cold water.
In the meantime, boil the milk in a pan. Peel the clove of garlic and leave to infuse in the hot milk – off the heat – for 15 minutes.

2 Place the cod in a pan of cold water. Heat and remove the fish fillet as soon as the water simmers. Leave to cool in a colander. Pre-heat the oven to 160°C/ 320°F.

3 Peel the cooked potato and roughly cut it up and place in a dish. Remove the clove of garlic from the milk and mash it and the potato with a fork.
Crumble in the cod and mix together. Adjust the seasoning. Put to one side.

4 Wash, dry and chop the parsley. In a round bottomed bowl, whisk the egg yolks, add the infused milk and chopped parsley. Whisk vigorously. Gradually pour the mixture into the mashed potato and cod, mixing together with a fork.

5 Share the mixture between the individual ovenproof dishes and place in a dish in the oven. Pour warm water in the dish up to ⅔ of the glasses height and place in the oven in a double boiler for 30 minutes.

6 Whilst they cook, peel and cut the vitelotte potato into thin slices using a mandoline or a peeler. Heat the oil in a pan and fry the vitelotte chips.
Use tongs to remove them and put to one side on some absorbent paper.
Remove the dishes from the oven, sprinkle with brown sugar and caramelize with the cooking torch. Decorate with a vitelotte chip. Serve straight away.

## Chef's tips

Cod is naturally salty; do not add any extra salt without tasting first.
If the cod is not desalted, do this the night before: Wash the filet in running water.
Place the fish on a grill and plunge into a large recipient of cold water (skin side up).
Change the water 2 to 3 times.

# Crème brûlée with cep mushrooms & herbs

## Ingredients

4 egg yolks

20cl/ 6 ¾ fl oz
semi-skimmed milk

20cl/ 6 ¾ fl oz single full fat
fresh cream

50g/ 1 ¾ oz dried
cep mushrooms

1 sprig flat parsley

1 sprig fresh coriander

2 tablespoons grapeseed oil

1 tablespoon brown sugar

Salt, ground black pepper


1 fine sieve

4 small glass jars or cocottes

**The day before :**

1 Warm the milk in a pan. Remove from heat and plunge the cep mushrooms into the milk.
Leave to infuse in the fridge overnight.

**On the day :**

2 Pre-heat the oven to 160°C/ 320°F.

3 Remove half the cep mushrooms and dice. Put to one side.
Mix the remaining mushrooms and the milk in a blender.
Pour through a fine sieve and put to one side.

4 In a round bottomed bowl, whisk the egg yolks, season with salt and pepper.
Add the mushroom-milk and stir thoroughly.
Gently add the cream and the diced cep mushrooms to the mixture.

5 Share the mixture between the jars or cocottes and place in a dish in the oven. Pour warm
water in the dish up to ⅔ of the jars' height and place in the oven in a double boiler
for 30 minutes.

6 Whilst they cook, remove the leaves from the parsley and coriander.
Heat the oil in a pan and fry the herbs.
Gently remove them with tongs and place on a piece of absorbent paper.

7 Remove from the oven, sprinkle with brown sugar and caramelize with the cooking torch.
Place the fried herbs over the crèmes brûlées and serve straight away.

4 people

preparation 20 mn

160°C Th 5 35 mn

difficulty ★ ★ ★

# Caramelized pork crème brûlée with coconut & cashew nuts

## Ingredients

4 egg yolks

20cl/ 6 ¾ fl oz semi-skimmed milk

20cl/ 6 ¾ fl oz coconut cream

200g/ 7 oz lean pork fillet

50g/ 1 ¾ oz granulated sugar

1 small shallot

1 sprig coriander

1 tablespoon olive oil

1 tablespoon cashew nuts

1 tablespoon brown sugar

Salt, ground pepper


4 deep ramekins

1  Pre-heat the oven to 160°C/ 320°F.
   Peel and chop the shallot. Chop the coriander. Cut the pork into very thin slices.

2  Pour a drizzle of olive oil in a pan and brown the shallot, on a low heat.
   Add the meat and brown on all sides.
   Sprinkle some granulated sugar over the top and leave to caramelize for a few moments.
   Put to one side.

3  In a round bottomed bowl, whisk the egg yolks with the salt and pepper.
   Add the coconut cream and the milk. Mix thoroughly. Gently add the chopped coriander.

4  Place the slices of caramelized pork in the bottom of the ramekins and cover
   with the mixture.
   Place the ramekins in a dish in the oven. Pour warm water in the dish up to ²/₃
   of the ramekins' height and place in the oven in a double boiler for 35 minutes.

5  Whilst they cook, heat a pan, without any oil, and roast the cashew nuts, stirring around
   continuously. Put to one side.

6  Remove from the oven, sprinkle with brown sugar and caramelize with the cooking torch.
   Sprinkle with roasted cashew nuts and serve straight away.

# Smoky bacon crème brûlée

## Ingredients

4 egg yolks

20cl/ 6 ¹/₄ fl oz
semi-skimmed milk

20cl/ 6 ¹/₄ fl oz single full fat
fresh cream

6 thin slices smoky bacon

4 sprigs chives

1 tablespoon brown sugar

Salt, ground pepper


1 fine sieve

4 ramekins or 16 mini-ramekins

1 Pre-heat the oven to 150°C/ 302°F.
Boil the milk in a pan.
Remove from heat, place 2 slices of smoky bacon inside and leave to infuse for 10 minutes.
Chop the chives.

2 Pour the milk and the 2 slices of bacon into a blender.
Mix thoroughly then pour through a fine sieve. Put to one side.

3 In a round bottomed bowl, whisk the egg yolks, season with salt and pepper.
Add the bacon-milk. Mix thoroughly.
Gently add the chives and fresh cream, being careful not to froth.

4 Share the mixture between the ramekins, place in the drip pan, pour some water inside
and place in the oven in a double boiler for 30 minutes for individual ramekins
or 15 minutes for the appetizers.

5 Whilst they cook, heat a pan, without any oil.
Cut the 4 slices of bacon into strips and cook on a low heat until they curl.
Gently remove them with tongs and place on a piece of absorbent paper.

6 Remove from the oven, sprinkle with brown sugar and caramelize with the cooking torch.
Place the strips of crispy bacon on top of the crèmes brulées and serve straight away.

# Crème brûlée with curried cauliflower & leek whisps

## Ingredients

4 egg yolks

20cl/ 6 ¾ fl oz semi-skimmed milk

20cl/ 6 ¾ fl oz single full fat fresh cream

100g/ 3 ½ oz cauliflower

1 clove pink garlic

1 leek (white only)

1 pinch curry powder

1 tablespoon sunflower oil

1 tablespoon brown sugar

Salt, ground pepper

1 fine sieve

4 ramekins

1 Pre-heat the oven to 160°C/ 320°F.
Boil a large pan of salted water.
Peel the garlic and grate its pulp. Put to one side.

2 Wash and cut the cauliflower into small pieces.
Place in the boiling, salted water and leave to cook for 10 minutes.
Using a colander, drain, then rinse in cold water.

3 Pour the milk in a blender. Add half the cauliflower and the grated garlic pulp.
Mix thoroughly then pour through a fine sieve.

4 In a round bottomed bowl, beat the egg yolks with the salt, pepper and curry powder.
Whisk in the cauliflower-milk. Gently add the fresh cream, without frothing.

5 Place the pieces of drained cauliflower at the bottom of the ramekins. Fill with
the mixture. Place in the drip pan, pour some water inside, up to ⅔ of the ramekins' height
and place in the oven in a double boiler for 30 minutes.

6 Whilst they cook, wash the leek whites and cut into juliennes, lengthways.
Heat the oil in a pan and quickly brown the leek whisps.
Pat with a piece of absorbent paper and put to one side.

7 Remove from the oven, place the leek whisps on top, then sprinkle with brown sugar
and caramelize with the cooking torch. Serve straight away.

## Chef's tips

Use the Mastrad multi-steamer to cook the cauliflower and cool off with cold water:
10 minutes over a pan, 5 minutes in the microwave.
Mastrad's garlic peeler and grater is ideal for grating the garlic.

4 people    preparation 20 mn     140°C Th 4 - 5 20 mn    difficulty ★ ★ ★

# Bouillabaisse-style crème brûlée

## Ingredients

4 egg yolks

20cl/ 6 ¾ fl oz semi-skimmed milk

20cl/ 6 ¾ fl oz single full fat fresh cream

75g/ 2 ¾ oz John Dory fish filet

75g/ 2 ¾ oz salmon filet

4 good size prawns

1 clove purple garlic

1 slice whole wheat bread

1 tablespoon olive oil

1 tablespoon brown sugar

1 pinch Cayenne pepper

1 pinch powdered saffron

Salt, ground pepper


4 ramekins deep or

small individual soup dishes

1   Pre-heat the oven to 140°C/ 284°F.
Peel the clove of garlic.

2   Warm the milk on a low heat in a pan with a pinch of saffron.
When it begins to simmer, remove from heat, pop the clove of garlic inside and leave to infuse for 10 minutes.

3   While this cooks, cut the fish filets into small pieces and shell the prawns.
Share the sea food between the ramekins. Put to one side.

4   In a round bottomed bowl, beat the egg yolks with the salt, pepper and Cayenne pepper.
Remove the garlic from the pan and pour the warm milk over the eggs, whisking as you do so. Gently add the cream to the mixture, without frothing.

5   Pour the mixture over the seafood, place the ramekins in an ovenproof dish.
Pour some warm water in the dish up to ⅔ of the ramekins' height and place in the oven in a double boiler for 20 minutes.

6   Whilst they cook, dice the bread into small pieces.
Heat the oil in a pan, brown the croutons then pat them with some absorbent paper. Put to one side.

7   Remove from the oven, sprinkle with brown sugar and caramelize with the cooking torch.
Sprinkle the croutons over the crèmes brulées. Serve straight away.

**4 people** | preparation **15 mn** | **160°C Th 5 30 mn** | difficulty ★ ★ ★

# Pumpkin crème brûlée, with crispy parmesan

## Ingredients

4 egg yolks

20cl/ 6¾ fl oz semi-skimmed milk

20cl/ 6¾ fl oz single full fat fresh cream

150g/ 5¼ oz pumpkin

50g/ 1¾ oz grated parmesan

1 teaspoon dried marjoram

1 tablespoon brown sugar

Olive oil

Salt, ground pepper

1 fine sieve

4 ramekins or deep bowls

1. Pre-heat the oven to 160°C/ 320°F.

2. Clean and cut the pumpkin into small pieces. Cook on a low heat in a pan with a drizzle of olive oil and the marjoram, stirring continuously, until you obtain a compote.

3. Pour the milk in a blender. Add the pumpkin and mix thoroughly. Pour through a sieve and put to one side.

4. In a round bottomed bowl, whisk the egg yolks, season with salt and pepper. Add the pumpkin-milk and stir thoroughly. Add the cream and half the parmesan, mixing gently.

5. Share the mixture between the ramekins then place them in an ovenproof dish. Pour some warm water in the dish up to ⅔ of the ramekins' height and place in the oven in a double boiler for 30 minutes.

6. Whilst they cook, heat a pan, without any oil. Using a spoon, place the remaining grated parmesan in 4 heaps in the hot pan. Turn them over using a silicone spatula and leave to brown for a few moments. Put on a plate.

7. Remove the crèmes from the oven, sprinkle with brown sugar and caramelize with the cooking torch. Top with a parmesan crisp and serve straight away.

## Chef's tips

Vary your culinary pleasures by using seasonal cucurbits found at the market.

# Desserts

The favourite dessert of the French: the crème brûlée!
It provides a plethora of variations to delight our palates!
Try your hand at these recipes and leave room for some creativity:
vanilla, chocolate, caramel, pistachio, blended fruits or in chunks, flower or tea infusions...
Sprinkled with brown sugar, coloured or flavoured sugars, dried fruits, crushed boiled sweets...
Caramelize with a cooking torch...and enjoy!

| 4 desserts | ou | 16 mini | preparation 10 mn leave to stand 2 h | desserts 100°C Th 3 50 mn | mini 100°C Th 3 25 mn | difficulty ★★★ |
|---|---|---|---|---|---|---|

# Sweet wine and walnut crème brûlée

## Ingredients

50cl/ 1 ¾ fl oz single full fat fresh cream

6 egg yolks

16 walnuts

100g/ 3 ½ oz caster sugar

10cl/ 3 ½ fl oz sweet white wine (Sauternes *)

2 tablespoons brown sugar or cane sugar


4 individual dishes
or 16 mini dishes

**1** Pre-heat the oven to 100°C/ 212°F.
Roughly chop the walnuts.

**2** In a round bottomed bowl, whisk the egg yolks with the caster sugar until they whiten.
Gradually pour the cream in, stirring continuously.
Add the sweet wine*, mix thoroughly.

**3** Share the mixture between the dishes and fill to ¾ of their height, then place in a drip pan. Pour some warm water in the pan up to ⅔ of the dishes' height and place in the oven in a double boiler for 50 minutes for the individual portions, 25 minutes for the mini portions.

**4** Remove from the oven and leave to cool at room temperature before putting in the fridge for at least 2 hours.

**5** Mix the chopped walnuts with the brown sugar.
Sprinkle this mixture over the crèmes when ready to serve and caramelize with a cooking torch.

## Chef's tips

This crème brûlée is the perfect accompaniment to a cheese platter.


* Excessive consumption of alcohol is dangerous to your health. Drink in moderation.

| 4 people | preparation 20 mn | | difficulty |
|---|---|---|---|
| | leave to stand 2 h | 90°C Th 3 40 mn | ★ ★ ★ |

# Vanilla and gingerbread crème brûlée

## Ingredients

6 egg yolks

60g/ 2 ½ oz caster sugar

40cl/ 13 ¼ fl oz single fresh cream

4 slices soft gingerbread

1 vanilla pod

4 teaspoons brown sugar


4 ramekins

1  Pre-heat the oven to 90°C/ 194°F.
   Split the vanilla pod in half. Remove the inside with a knife.

2  Pour the cream in a pan.
   Add 30g/ 1 ⅛ oz caster sugar and the vanilla grains.
   Bring to the boil, stirring as you do so.
   Remove from heat as it starts to boil and leave to cool.

3  In a round bottomed bowl, whisk the egg yolks and the remaining 30g/ 1 ⅛ oz
   of caster sugar, until it whitens.
   Gradually add the vanilla-cream to the whitened eggs, and mix gently.

4  Cut the slices of soft gingerbread into small cubes and spread them over the bottom
   of the ramekins.
   Cover the gingerbread with the vanilla- cream mixture.

5  Place the ramekins in an ovenproof dish. Pour some water in the dish up to ⅔
   of the ramekins' height and place in the oven in a double boiler for 40 minutes.

6  Leave the ramekins to cool at room temperature before putting in the fridge for at least
   2 hours.

7  When ready to serve, sprinkle with brown sugar and caramelize with the cooking torch.

4 desserts ou 16 mini oven

preparation 20 mn
leave to stand 2 h

desserts
160°C Th 5
25 mn

mini oven
160°C Th 5
12 mn

difficulty
★ ★ ★

# Violet crème brûlée

## Ingredients

6 egg yolks

20cl/ 6³/₄ fl oz
semi-skimmed milk

20cl/ 6³/₄ single full fat
fresh cream

60g/ 2 ¹/₄ oz fine caster sugar

1 tablespoon violet essence

1 tablespoon crystallized
violet petals

2 tablespoons brown sugar

4 individual ramekins
or 16 mini ramekins

1   Pre-heat the oven to 160°C/ 320°F.
Pour the milk and cream into a pan.
Heat on a very low flame, stirring constantly. Remove from heat.

2   In a round bottomed bowl, whisk the egg yolks and sugar until the mixture whitens.

3   Add the warm milk-cream mix to the whitened eggs little by little, stirring gently with
a silicone spoon, without frothing.
Add the violet essence and mix gently.

4   Share the mixture between the ramekins and place the ramekins in an ovenproof dish.
Pour some warm water in the dish up to ²/₃ of the ramekins' height and place in the oven in
a double boiler for 25 minutes for the individual ramekins, 12 minutes for
the mini ramekins.

5   Remove the ramekins from the oven and leave to cool.
Put them in the fridge for at least 2 hours.

6   When ready to serve, sprinkle the crèmes brûlées with brown sugar and the crystallized
violet petals. Caramelize with the cooking torch and serve straight away.

## Chef's tips

Vary the flavours by using other flower essences: rose, lavender, poppy,
orange-flower water...

| | | | | | | |
|---|---|---|---|---|---|---|
| **4** desserts | ou | **16** mini | preparation **30 mn** leave to stand **2 h** | desserts 150°C Th 5 **30 mn** | mini 150°C Th 5 **15 mn** | difficulty ★ ★ ★ |

# Creamy chestnut crème brûlée

## Ingredients

4 egg yolks

2 chestnuts, uncooked or pre-cooked

15cl/ 5 fl oz semi-skimmed milk

25cl/ 8 ½ fl oz full fat single fresh cream

50g/ 1 ¾ oz granulated sugar

½ vanilla pod

4 teaspoons chestnut cream

2 tablespoons brown sugar


1 fine sieve

4 ovenproof glasses
or 16 small ovenproof glasses

**1**  If using uncooked chestnuts, peel and score them with a knife.
Place in a pan of cold water and bring to the boil. Cook for 15 minutes.

**2**  Pour the milk in a pan. Place the vanilla and the cooked (or pre-cooked chestnuts) inside and simmer. Leave to infuse for 15 minutes, then remove the vanilla.

**3**  Pre-heat the oven to 150°C/ 302°F.
Mix the chestnuts and the milk with an electric hand blender.
Pour through a fine sieve and put to one side.

**4**  In a round bottomed bowl, whisk the egg yolks with the granulated sugar until the mixture whitens. Add the chestnut-milk and stir thoroughly.
Add the fresh cream and mix gently.

**5**  Put a teaspoon of chestnut cream into each glass then fill with the mixture.
Place the ramekins in a drip pan. Pour some water in the pan up to ²/₃ of the ramekins' height and place in the oven in a double boiler for 30 minutes for the individual desserts, 15 minutes for the mini-desserts.

**6**  Remove the crèmes from the oven and leave to cool at room temperature before putting in the fridge for at least 2 hours.

**7**  When ready to serve, sprinkle with brown sugar and caramelize with a cooking torch.

## Chef's tips

The chestnuts can be cooked in a Mastrad multi-steamer, for 15 minutes over a pan of boiling water.

# Candied orange and lemon crème brûlée

## Ingredients

50cl/ 17 fl oz full fat milk

1 orange

1 lemon

60g/ 2 ¼ oz ground almonds

5 egg yolks

1 teaspoon flour

80g/ 2 ¾ oz fine caster sugar

10g/ ¼ oz candied lemon

10g/ ¼ oz candied orange

1 tablespoon orange-flower water

4 individual ramekins
or 16 mini ramekins

1   Pre-heat the oven to 180°C/ 356°F.

2   In a pan, warm the milk on a low heat.
In the meantime, dice the fruit.
Wash and dry the orange and lemon. Remove a teaspoon of the zest from
both citrus fruits.

3   In a round bottomed bowl, mix the ground almonds with the egg yolks, 50g/ 1 ¾ oz sugar,
the lemon and orange zests, the diced, candied fruit and the flour.
Gradually add the hot milk, stirring continuously until the mixture is smooth.

4   Pour the mixture in a pan and cook on a low heat for 10 minutes, stirring continuously
with a silicone spoon.
Remove the cream from the heat as soon as it begins to thicken and stir in
the orange-flower water.

5   Share the mixture between the ramekins. Place the ramekins in a drip pan. Pour some
water in the pan up to ½ the ramekins' height and place in the oven in a double boiler
for 8 minutes for the individual creams, 4 minutes pour les mini-creams.

6   Remove the ramekins from the oven and leave to cool at room temperature.

7   When ready to serve, sprinkle the ramekins with sugar and caramelize with
the cooking torch.

## Chef's tips
Use organic citrus fruits.

| 4 desserts | ou | 16 mini oven | preparation 10 mn leave to stand 2 h | desserts 150°C Th 5 30 mn | mini oven 150°C Th 5 15 mn | difficulty ★ ★ ★ |

# Pistachio crème brûlée with caramelized fruit sweets

## Ingredients

4 egg yolks

20cl/ 6 ¾ fl oz semi-skimmed milk

20cl/ 6 ¾ fl oz single full fat fresh cream

40g/ 1 ¼ oz granulated sugar

3 teaspoons unsalted pistachios

2 fruit flavoured boiled sweets

1 fine sieve

4 individual ramekins or 16 mini ramekins

1 Pre-heat the oven to 150°C/ 302°F.
Shell the pistachios and keep ⅓ for decoration.

2 Pour the milk in a pan. Add the pistachios and the sugar.
Bring to the boil, stirring as you do so.
Mix with an electric hand mixer and pour through a fine sieve. Put to one side.

3 In a round bottomed bowl, whisk the egg yolks and the fresh cream.
Gently add the pistachio-milk, stirring as you do so.

4 Fill the ramekins and place them in a drip pan. Pour some water in the pan and place in the oven in a double boiler: for 30 minutes for the individual desserts, 15 minutes for the mini-desserts.

5 Remove from the oven and leave to cool at room temperature before putting in the fridge for at least 2 hours.

**5 minutes before serving :**

6 Heat a pan, without any oil and roast the remaining pistachios.
Use a chopper or a mortar to crush the boiled sweets to obtain a powder.
Sprinkle the crèmes brulées with the ground sweets and caramelize with a cooking torch.
Use to decorate the desserts along with the pistachios.

**6 people** | preparation **20 mn** | 160°C Th 5 **20 mn** | difficulty ★ ★ ★

# Blackcurrant crème brûlée

## Ingredients

8 egg yolks

30cl/ 10 fl oz full fat milk

70cl/ 23 ½ fl oz thick fresh cream

600g/ 1lb ¼ oz fresh or frozen blackcurrants

200g/ 7 oz caster sugar

1 vanilla pod

3 tablespoons brown sugar

1 fine sieve

6 deep ramekins
or ovenproof glasses

1 Rinse (or defrost) the blackcurrants.
Pre-heat the oven to 160°C/ 320°F.

2 Split the vanilla pod in half. Remove the inside with a knife to recuperate
the grains and flesh.

3 Pour the milk in a pan and put the vanilla flesh and grains inside, along with
300g/ 10 ½ oz blackcurrants. Bring to simmering point on a medium heat, stirring gently.
Leave to simmer for 10 minutes.

4 In the meantime, in a round bottomed bowl, whisk the egg yolks and the caster sugar until
the mixture whitens. Add the fresh cream and stir thoroughly.

5 Pour the blackcurrant-milk in a blender. Mix thoroughly then pour through a fine sieve.
Gradually whisk the blackcurrant-milk into the mixture in the round bottomed bowl.

6 Share the 300g/ 10 ½ oz of blackcurrants between the ramekins and fill with the mixture.
Place them in a drip pan. Pour some water in the pan, up to ⅔ of the height of
the ramekins and place in the oven in a double boiler for 20 minutes.

7 Remove from the oven, sprinkle the brown sugar over the top and caramelize with
a cooking torch and serve straight away.

## Chef's tips
Eat the desserts whilst warm.

4 people

preparation
15 mn

leave to stand
2 h

100°C Th 3
60 mn

difficulty
★ ★ ★

# Green tea crème brûlée with crunchy pistachio topping

## Ingredients

10cl/ 3 ¼ fl oz
semi-skimmed milk

50cl/ 17 fl oz fresh single, full
cream

6 egg yolks

100g/ 3 ½ oz granulated sugar

3 tablespoons brown sugar

1 tablespoon green tea powder

2 tablespoons unsalted
pistachio nuts

4 ovenproof ceramic cups
or ovenproof glasses

1   Pre-heat the oven to 100°C/ 212°F.

2   Boil the milk in a pan.
As soon as it boils, remove from heat and add the green tea.
Leave to infuse for 5 minutes.

3   Add the fresh cream and warm on a low heat for 10 minutes, stirring regularly with
a silicone spoon.

4   In a round bottomed bowl, whisk the egg yolks and the granulated sugar until
the mixture whitens.

5   Gradually pour the cream-tea mixture over the whitened eggs, stirring as you do so.
Mix thoroughly.

6   Share the cream between the ovenproof cups and place in a baking tray.
Pour some water in the tray, up to ⅔ of the height of the cups and place in the oven
in a double boiler for 1 hour.

7   Shell and crush the pistachios. Brown them in a pan without any oil. Put to one side.

8   Remove the crèmes from the oven, leave to cool at room temperature then place
in the fridge for at least 2 hours.

9   When ready to server, sprinkle the crèmes with the crushed pistachios and brown sugar.
Caramelize with a cooking torch and eat straight away.

| 4 desserts | ou | 16 mini oven | preparation 15 mn leave to stand 2 h | desserts 120°C Th 4 20 mn | mini oven 120°C Th 4 10 mn | difficulty ★★★ |

# Chocolate and peppercorn crème brûlée

## Ingredients

10cl/ 3 ¼ fl oz fresh single cream

125ml/ 4 ½ fl oz semi-skimmed milk

40g/ 1 ½ oz dark chocolate (70% cocoa content)

50g/ 1 ¾ oz caster sugar

2 egg yolks

2 tablespoons cane sugar

Whole peppercorns to grind


4 individual ramekins
or 16 mini ramekins

**1** Pre-heat the oven to 120°C.
Chop the chocolate into small pieces.

**2** Heat the milk in a pan. Remove from heat and add all the chocolate at once.
Wait 30 seconds and whisk the mixture until all the chocolate has melted.

**3** In a round bottomed bowl, mix the egg yolks with the caster sugar until the mixture whitens. Whisk the whitened eggs into the chocolate-milk mixture.
Stir the fresh cream in gently. Add a twist of ground pepper.

**4** Share the mixture between the ramekins and put them in an ovenproof dish.
Pour some water in the dish, up to ²/₃ of the height of the ramekins and place in the oven in a double boiler for 20 minutes for the individual desserts, 10 minutes for the mini-desserts.

**5** Leave the crèmes to cool then place in the fridge for at least 2 hours.

**6** When ready to serve, lightly sprinkle the cane sugar over the top and caramelize with a cooking torch.

## Chef's tips

The chocolate flavour is enhanced by the pepper. Any type of pepper can be used except the 5 pepper mixture (black pepper, white pepper, green pepper, pink peppercorns and Jamaican pepper). This mini-dessert is perfect for a gourmet coffee break.

A lot of hard work, pleasure and a great team spirit went into making this book !

We hope you have as much fun making these crèmes brûlées with our cooking torches.

**To all Mastrad clients and avid readers of our first recipe books :**

Thank you for your delicious feed back and your loyalty which encourages us to strive to serve you even better.

**To Jean-Claude, the cream of the crop!**

Thank you for keeping the flame alive! And thank you for sharing the secrets of the association of oh so creamy cream and crunchy toppings... absolutely delicious !

**To Julien, «the Jolly Green Giant»:**

Under the fiery exterior lies a soft centre... thank you for putting these incredible contrasts and textures in the spotlight!

**To Yul Studio:**

Thank you for your efficiency! Professional tools that provide a delightful result, in record time!

**To Mastrad's Marketing team:**

Thank you for your eager participation!

© 2010 Mastrad
Mastrad Essentials Collection – Crèmes Brûlées
ISSN : 1968-8245
ISBN : 978-2-9531963-6-8
Registration of Copyright: September 2010
Printing completed September 2010 by Xinlian
Artistic Printing Cie / China

Mastrad SA
32bis - 34 , Boulevard de Picpus
75012 Paris
FRANCE
Tél : +33 (1) 49 26 96 00
Fax : +33 (1) 49 26 96 06
www.mastrad.fr